Original title:
Life's Meaning: I'm Pretty Sure It's Ice Cream

Copyright © 2025 Creative Arts Management OÜ
All rights reserved.

Author: Vivienne Beaumont
ISBN HARDBACK: 978-1-80566-258-7
ISBN PAPERBACK: 978-1-80566-553-3

Creamy Conversations

In a cone of dreams we sit,
Chasing sprinkles, never quit.
Truths unfold with every scoop,
Laughter's swirled in creamy hoops.

Melting hearts in summer days,
I scream for joy in silly ways.
Conversations licked like treats,
Joyful noise, our hearts, it beats.

Lessons from the Scoop

Two scoops of wisdom piled high,
Waffle cone thoughts that wave goodbye.
Don't rush, savor each sweet taste,
Life's a feast, no time to waste.

Chocolate chips and cherry swirls,
Sprinkled dreams for boys and girls.
In every flavor, lessons found,
In every bite, pure joy unbound.

An Ode to Every Flavor

Vanilla, mint, or rocky road,
In each cone, a story flowed.
Nutty bliss and fruit-filled hopes,
Every scoop, a way to cope.

Caramel swirls and fudge-filled skies,
Life's a buffet of tasty pies.
Every flavor's a little joke,
Savoring each, as laughter's bespoke.

Frosted Wishes

Underneath the starlit night,
Cup in hand, it feels so right.
Frosted wishes gently gleam,
In chocolate, life's but a dream.

Dripping joy from each delight,
From cookie dough to berry bright.
Wishing wells not made of stone,
Just scoop it up, you're not alone.

The Joyful Scoop

In a cone so sweet and tall,
Melting dreams begin to fall.
Chocolate rivers, sprinkles bright,
Laughter echoes, pure delight.

Sundaes dance on sunny days,
Fudge and nuts in joyful ways.
Waffle cups and flavors rare,
Happiness is everywhere!

Every scoop, a giggle shared,
A creamy world, we are all spared.
For spry delight, we can't resent,
In frozen joy, we find content.

So let us eat, without a care,
The joy of sweets, forever fair.
In playful bites, we find our cheer,
With every scoop, the world's more clear.

Delight Served Cold

Beneath the sun, we gather round,
A frosty treat, so glory-bound.
Rainbow swirls and cherry tops,
Laughter bursts, the sweetness pops.

Epic cones that tower high,
Like golden dreams that touch the sky.
Sticky fingers, joyous shouts,
In every bite, the fun just sprouts.

Worry not, let laughter flow,
As chocolate drips, our spirits glow.
With every spoon, a reason found,
In every bowl, pure joy abounds.

So stack those scoops and dig right in,
The day begins, let laughter win.
In chilly bliss, we seize the day,
With every scoop, we shout hooray!

The Flavor of Now

In the scoop of today, oh so bright,
Chocolate swirls dance in pure delight.
Sprinkles of laughter, a cherry on top,
In this moment, I never want to stop.

With every cold lick, the joy I find,
Melting away the worries behind.
Waffle cones cradling all of my hopes,
Savoring flavors, we're all just dope.

Whispers of Vanilla Dreams

Beneath the stars, on a summer's night,
Vanilla whispers, oh what a sight!
Each creamy bite, a sweet serenade,
In this tasty dream, we're never afraid.

Silliness drips down our chins, so free,
Kicking our shoes off, just you and me.
In a world of flavors, we twirl and spin,
Chasing each giggle, let the fun begin!

Cones of Hope and Happiness

A scoop of sunshine in every cone,
Joy sprinkles bright, never alone.
Together we laugh, we savor the bliss,
In the frozen moment, life doesn't miss.

Mixing flavors like a painter's brush,
Creating a masterpiece, what a rush!
With each joyful scoop, the troubles subside,
In cones of hope, let happiness ride.

The Taste of Tomorrow

With flavors unknown waiting in line,
I scoop up tomorrow, it tastes divine!
Minty freshness, a promise to keep,
In a world of scoops, I happily leap.

Future so sweet, like a sundae surprise,
With every sweet bite, I reach for the skies.
Chasing the flavors that dance in my mind,
In the delicious tomorrow, happiness binds.

Echoes of Vanilla Vows

In a cone, our dreams reside,
With sprinkles of joy, we take a ride.
Chocolate rivers flow with glee,
Whipped cream clouds, just you and me.

Every scoop, a memory made,
In sweet delight, our worries fade.
With cherry tops on life's carousel,
We laugh as flavors weave their spell.

The Carousel of Confections

Swirling colors, a joyful dance,
Each scoop brings us a second chance.
In every flavor, giggles bloom,
A symphony of taste to consume.

Minty moments, wild and bright,
In a sundae kiss, we feel the light.
Cotton candy dreams swirl high,
As chocolate kisses float on by.

When Happiness Drips

A cone tips over—oh, what a mess!
But laughter rises, no need to stress.
With every drip, a story to tell,
In sticky moments, we wear joy well.

Cotton clouds high, we dance with cheer,
When life gets messy, we persevere.
Scoop by scoop, we conquer strife,
A world of sweet in this ice cream life.

A Scoop of Thoughtfulness

In shiny shops, we gather round,
With creamy wonders that astound.
A scoop of kindness, piled high,
With chocolate hugs, we'll never cry.

Sprinkled thoughts, like stars above,
In bowls of laughter, we find our love.
With every bite, our hearts unwind,
In frosty moments, joy we find.

Scoop of Existence

In the bowl of joy we find,
A scoop to soothe the weary mind.
Each flavor bursts like laughter's sound,
In creamy swirls, our bliss is found.

Chocolate curls, a nutty cheer,
Vanilla dreams with every tear.
Sprinkles dance, a colorful spree,
In this sweet world, we roam so free.

Sweet Melodies in a Cone

Notes of fudge, a musical treat,
Each bite is like a rhythmic beat.
Melodies swirl in a crispy shell,
A candy chorus that sings so well.

With every taste, the laughter flows,
Beneath warm sun, the happiness grows.
Together we sing, a joyous refrain,
For in our cones, there's no more pain.

Flavorful Whispers of Joy

A whisper of berry, a dash of glee,
Life's secrets hidden in flavors we see.
Every spoonful tells a tale,
Of childhood summers and laughter trails.

Minty surprises and crunchy bits,
In our hearts, that sweetness sits.
We trade our woes for a sugary smile,
In this creamy dream, let's stay awhile.

The Cream that Dreams

Under the stars, we share a treat,
The cream that dreams is oh so sweet.
In joyous scoops, our worries fade,
As laughter and flavors serenely parade.

A dash of humor, a sprinkle of fun,
We taste the moments as they run.
With every lick, the world seems right,
In this frozen bliss, we take our flight.

Beneath the Soft Serve Sky

Under whipped clouds, I drift and dream,
Sprinkles fall like stars, or so it seems.
A scoop of chaos in a cone so tall,
Each bite's a giggle, I could have it all.

Sunshine melts the worries from my mind,
With flavors mixed, the perfect blend I find.
Chocolate rivers flow, happiness on cue,
Amidst this frosty joy, I laugh anew.

Surreal Swirls of Serenity

In a world where swirls collide and dance,
Minty fresh moments spark a silly prance.
Cherry top hats on chocolate tummies,
Here, life is sweeter, never too crummy.

Unicorns serve scoops with rainbow spoons,
Cowboys ride dips beneath the cheese moon.
Beneath this creamy sky, I leap with glee,
Each lick, a treasure; a scoop, the key.

Chilled Reflections in a Cup

In my frosty chalice, dreams reflect,
With each cold sip, I can disconnect.
Whispers of waffle cones dance on my tongue,
Tickling these thoughts, laughter's just begun.

Sundaes float on the waves of delight,
Twirling in rhythms, oh what a sight!
Coconut flakes glide like birds in flight,
While gummy bears keep the giggles bright.

Taste Buds and Timeless Moments

Every scoop tells tales of days gone by,
Of sticky fingers and sweet alibis.
A dribble of syrup down my chin,
Moments like these get under my skin.

S'more laughter joins marshmallow delight,
Crispy crumbs mimic stars on a night.
This flavor fiesta fills my heart's space,
In the land of treats, I've found my place.

Sweet Escapades

In a cone or cup, it calls my name,
Every scoop of joy, never the same.
Sprinkles dance like confetti bright,
In this chilled world, everything's right.

Chocolate rivers, a caramel stream,
Waffles that wink, oh what a dream!
With every lick, the worries flee,
A sweet escape, just you and me.

A Bowl Full of Dreams

A bowl of wonder, colors collide,
Nuts and cherries, a joyful ride.
With each swirl, my frown disappears,
These frosty treats banish all fears.

Mountains of whipped, so light and airy,
Festive and frosty, nothing's too scary.
Savor the scoop, let troubles drift,
In this chilled realm, my spirits lift.

The Dessert of Existence

Oh, creamy delight, you've got my heart,
With flavors that play a delicious part.
Minty whispers, chocolatey dreams,
In every bite, joy lightly gleams.

Sundaes twinkle like stars at night,
Each spoonful dances, oh what a sight!
Banana splits grinning, life feels so grand,
This dessert of existence, perfectly planned.

Melodies of Mint

Chilled notes of mint, a symphony bright,
Dancing on taste buds, a pure delight.
Melodies swirl in a bowl of cheer,
With every taste, laughter draws near.

Fudgey sonnets and strawberry rhymes,
Each scoop, a story that twists and climbs.
In every flavor, a jolly refrain,
Life's playful tune, it's never mundane.

The Language of Sprinkles

In a world of sweet delight,
Sprinkles dance, oh what a sight!
Chocolate chips and whipped cream swirl,
Each scoop is a treasure to unfurl.

Life is a cone, stacked up high,
With every lick, I'm floating by.
Toppings galore, a rainbow hum,
Happiness found in a perfect crumb.

A Sundae of Solitude

When the world outside feels cold and gray,
I grab my spoon, and I'm on my way.
A cherry on top of thoughts so deep,
Sundaes cure those blues, I keep.

With fudge rivers flowing, I sit in glee,
My thoughts melt away, just like the spree.
Alone but not lonely, I savor now,
This moment of joy, it's my solemn vow.

Frosted Hopes and Melting Fears

In a bowl of dreams, fears take a dip,
With frosty hopes, let the laughter rip.
The more I scoop, the more I find,
That smiles can melt the grumpiest mind.

In waffle cups, my worries swirl,
With every bite, my thoughts unfurl.
Sprinkled laughter on a frosty day,
Ice cream therapy, come what may.

Cone of Contentment

In a cone filled with joy, I take a bite,
Every flavor sings, it feels just right.
Caramel swirls and toffee dreams,
Life's simple pleasures are sweeter than it seems.

So here's to scoops of pure delight,
With every crunch, my heart takes flight.
I chase my worries with a chocolate swirl,
In this cone of contentment, I'm ready to twirl.

Etched in Chocolate

In a cone I find my cheer,
Wobbling while I persevere.
More sprinkles, please, not too much stress,
Sweet moments here, I feel so blessed.

When the world feels cold and stark,
I search for joy, a sugary spark.
In flavors wild, I seek my peace,
With every scoop, my worries cease.

Life melts easy like a fudge,
A swirling mix, I'll never budge.
Chocolate chips, they'll lead the way,
Through gooey paths, I'll laugh and play.

So here's to joys in every bite,
A comedy of tastes, pure delight.
With spoons in hand, we all collide,
In this dessert, I take my ride.

A Universe of Toppings

In the galaxy of sweet delights,
Every topping brings pure heights.
Marshmallow fluff and cherry bliss,
Each scoop is like a little kiss.

Crushed cookies falling like stardust,
In this bowl, there's so much trust.
Whipped cream swirls like clouds above,
In this universe, I find my love.

Sprinkle rainbows on my treat,
With each bite, I find my beat.
Banana slices, nuts a'plenty,
Eating here, I feel quite fancy.

So grab a spoon and take your shot,
In a world where happiness is caught.
Let flavors dance with every scoop,
Come join the laughter in this group.

The Symphony of Sundaes

Hear the music in each bowl,
A symphony that makes me whole.
With every scoop, a note is sung,
Sundaes sweet, forever young.

Fudge cascades in slippery slides,
A melody my taste buds ride.
Cherries on top, they play their part,
Creating harmonies that warm the heart.

Peanut butter swirls around the beat,
A crunchy rhythm, oh so sweet.
Life's little joys, they serenade,
In every flavor, sweetness laid.

So let us gather for this show,
With joyous bites, our spirits grow.
The symphony of spoon and cheer,
In every sundae, love draws near.

Churned Realities

In the churner of my dreams,
Ice cream flows like sunny beams.
Peanut brittle, minty thrills,
Every flavor, joy fulfills.

Twists and turns of the ice cream dance,
Life's a scoop, just take the chance.
From waffle cones to chocolate fudge,
Each tasty bite, I'll never budge.

Flavor explosions, laughter spills,
Churned realities give us chills.
With friends beside, it's time to feast,
In this moment, worries ceased.

So laugh aloud, and scoop it high,
A world of cream beneath the sky.
In every cone, sweet truths we find,
With every scoop, we leave behind.

The Creamy Canvas

In a world of swirls and sprinkles,
Joy drips down in gooey twinkles.
Chocolate rivers, a cherry on top,
Art of dessert that never can stop.

A scoop of laughter, a scoop of glee,
Melt with a friend, just you and me.
Every flavor tells a silly tale,
A creamy journey, we cannot fail.

The cone's our guide, a crunchy friend,
In this sweet ride, there's no end.
Taste buds giggle, and hearts collide,
In this creamy canvas, we take a ride.

With every bite, a giggle breaks,
For silly moments, the heart awakes.
So let's indulge, let our worries freeze,
In this frosty fun, we feel the ease.

The Meltdown of Meaning

A scoop of confusion, oh, how it drips,
Life melts away between our sips.
Sticky fingers and wobbling cones,
Searching for depth in milkshake tones.

Laughter erupts as flavors clash,
Sprinkles fly in a silly splash.
Waffle wonders and silly shouts,
Finding wisdom in silly doubts.

A cherry gap of wise reflection,
Slipping along, we seek connection.
The laughter flows as ice cream does,
Finding clarity in about-what-was.

So face the heat and don't you fret,
For a frosty cone is the best pet.
As drips may fall, we wipe and cheer,
In melted moments, we draw near.

Cone-shaped Epiphanies

With every lick, a thought ignites,
In creamy textures, wisdom delights.
A cone of wonder, a scoop of dreams,
Dishing out joy in joyful themes.

Oops, I spilled my hopes and schemes,
Life's a sundae, bursting at the seams.
Flavors collide, a silly bite,
Epiphanies come in twilight's light.

Syrups swirl like thoughts in head,
With giggles and ice cream, there's no dread.
Scooping memories, a dash of fun,
In this cone-shaped quest, we've just begun.

So grab a spoon, let's taste the vibes,
In every bite, silly joy describes.
Life's delicious, just take it slow,
In cones of epiphanies, we grow.

Nostalgia in a Dish

Remember those days of frosty scoops,
In vibrant colors, we were little goops.
The ice cream truck's sweet, jingling sound,
Brings back the joy that knows no bound.

Peanut butter swirls and cookie bites,
Dancing in memories, sweet delights.
A dish of laughter, a sprinkle of cheer,
In every scoop, childhood's near.

As we dig deep, we cherish each taste,
Each lick a memory, never in haste.
Melted smiles drip like time does flee,
In this dish of joy, forever we'll be.

So here's to the past, the flavors that stuck,
In every cone of joy, we've all got luck.
Savoring nostalgia, let's share a dish,
In the creamy forever, we find our wish.

Frosty Footprints

In the cone of joy we tread,
Waffle paths where dreams are fed.
Sprinkles dance in sweet delight,
Every scoop a snowy bite.

Chasing circles, round and round,
In every flavor, laughter's found.
Chocolate rivers, minty streams,
Savoring our frosty dreams.

Spheres of Whimsy

Round and round, the flavors spin,
With a cherry on top, let's begin.
Laughter bubbles, joy will rise,
In every swirl, a tasty surprise.

Giggles pop like bubblegum,
In this land, who could feel glum?
Each lick a smile, a reason to cheer,
Joy served cold, we hold it dear.

The Essence of Enjoyment

Giggles melt in a sunny scoop,
Chasing taste, we form a troop.
Sticky fingers, joyful grins,
In this treat, the fun begins!

Fudge flows like a waterfall,
Together, we can have it all.
In every bowl, a spark of glee,
A creamy hug for you and me.

Drizzles of Delight

Syrups swirl in vibrant lines,
Each drop, a smile that brightly shines.
Laughter echoes, sweet and bright,
Creamy wonders, a pure delight.

With every bite, the world feels right,
Cones held high, we take flight.
Merry moments, a tasty jam,
In the swirl of cream, we say, "Yam!"

Flavors of the Heart

In a world that swirls like a scoop so bold,
Chocolate dreams and stories untold.
Strawberry whispers in every cone,
Laughs mixed in, never alone.

Minty adventures in every bite,
Cherry tops glimmering, oh what a sight!
Life's quirks blend like sprinkles on top,
We gather 'round, never want to stop.

Lemon zests that tickle and tease,
Whipped cream clouds floating with ease,
Each flavor a smile, a giggle, a song,
In this sweet bliss, we all belong.

So here's to the flavors, wild and free,
Every scoop a hint of glee.
With each tasty trial, we take part,
It's the laughter that flavors the heart.

Frozen Fantasies

In the freezer's glow, delights await,
Beneath frosty lids, we conjure fate.
Vanilla dreams blend with wild churn,
A swirl of joy, you'll never spurn.

Catch me in a waffle cone's embrace,
Each bite is a chuckle in this sweet race.
Buttery blends and cookies divine,
With each lick, the suns brightly shine.

Cherry explosions taste like a thrill,
A mountain of fudge, can't get my fill.
Sundae my troubles, oh chocolate galore,
In these frozen fantasies, I want more.

Even on days when the skies are gray,
A scoop of happiness leads the way.
With sprinkles of laughter, we share our dreams,
Together we savor life's creamy themes.

A Tasting of Togetherness

Gathered 'round with joyful glee,
Sampling flavors, just you and me.
Tasting spoonfuls, a delightful spree,
Every scoop whispers, "Set your heart free!"

Pistachio giggles and coconut sighs,
Sipping sweet shakes beneath sunny skies.
Banana splits, a friendship feast,
On this cone of laughter, we are the least.

Every flavor a laugh, a shared delight,
Tasting together feels just right.
With whipped dreams and bright sprinkles spread,
In this dish of joy, let's make our bed.

So here's to the moments, both silly and sweet,
In this tasting of love, we find our beat.
In every scoop, no need for distress,
Together we flourish, a true happiness.

The Sweet and Savory Journey

Traveling far on this creamy road,
A journey of laughter, a glorious ode.
From rocky roads to the fresh mint chase,
In this treat of delight, we find our place.

Savoring fudge like a joyride spree,
With every taste, we feel so carefree.
Odd flavors combine, a whimsical mix,
In a bowl of absurd, we find our fix.

Salty or sweet, who cares today?
Every spoonful sweeps worries away.
From birthday cakes to fruity spritz,
In this sweet journey, we're all misfits.

So grab a cone, throw caution in air,
In this joyful scoop, we haven't a care.
With laughter and flavors that twirl and play,
Together, we savor this zany buffet!

Melts in the Heart

When happiness scoops up in a cone,
We taste the joy, never alone.
With sprinkles dancing on top, so bright,
Every bite feels just so right.

Laughter bubbles with every churn,
For sweet delights, our hearts do yearn.
When troubles melt, like ice on sun,
A creamy feast, the best kind of fun.

Colorful tubs line the way,
Each flavor calls for a cheerful play.
A scoop of laughter, a dash of cheer,
Ice cream dreams bring loved ones near.

In every scoop, a story told,
Of friends united, both young and old.
With every lick, the world feels right,
A frozen joy, pure delight.

Dreams Served Cold

In a bowl or cone, sweet dreams reside,
Chillin' with fudge, they sip and slide.
With each cream swirl, worries fade away,
Spoonfuls of joy brighten our day.

Chocolate rivers, a caramel sea,
Tasting happiness, wild and free.
We gather 'round for a frozen treat,
Melodies of laughter, oh what a feat!

Every scoop a delightful fight,
Strawberry giggles, minty bites.
In our hearts, a cool breeze blows,
With flavors that tickle, joy overflows.

So grab a scoop, don't be shy,
In this creamy world, let's all fly high.
A cherry on top, a marshmallow cheer,
Let's dig in deep, our journey is here.

Essence of Euphoria

A swirl of colors in every dish,
Sprinkled with laughter, oh what a wish.
The essence of joy in every bowl,
A frozen hug for the happy soul.

Banana splits that twirl and dance,
With every crunch, we take a chance.
To share a smile, or perhaps two,
A tasty adventure awaits, so true.

A scoop of joy, a dash of fun,
Every bite shines brighter than the sun.
Fingers sticky but hearts so light,
In this creamy world, everything's right.

Life's a party, let's dive right in,
With cones held high, we're sure to win.
Laughter echoes, and flavors sing,
In the essence of joy, we find our spring.

Scoops of Sentiment

Scoops stacked high in a candy land,
With every flavor crafted by hand.
Those frosty smiles, such icy treats,
A scoop of love that never retreats.

Nostalgia blended with whipped cream delight,
We tasted memories in each sweet bite.
Conversations melt as we dig in deep,
A bond over ice cream, forever we'll keep.

Each cone a canvas, every swirl a dream,
With flavors that dance like a glistening beam.
Chocolate, vanilla, or bubblegum bliss,
In a world of scoops, who could resist?

So let's gather 'round with our bowls all bright,
In this silly journey, we take a big bite.
With giggles and grins, our hearts will expand,
Scoops of sentiment, oh isn't life grand?

Sweet Truths in a Dish

In a bowl of colors, secrets hide,
Each scoop of joy, a thrilling ride.
Chocolate dreams and vanilla plays,
Melt away troubles in sunny rays.

Sprinkles on top, a dance so grand,
Savor the moments, ice cream in hand.
Life's sweeter joys drip down the side,
Let laughter and ice cream be our guide.

Cravings for Connection

When the world feels cold on a rainy day,
A cone in my hand makes it all okay.
Sharing flavors, tales unfold,
Friendships grow like ice cream cold.

Taste buds tingle, smiles take flight,
Scooping joy from morning to night.
With every flavor, a bond we weave,
In silly moments, we truly believe.

A Tasty Journey Within

Sundaes and giggles, a wild delight,
Exploring the depths of each tasty bite.
Caramel swirls in a world so grand,
Discovering flavors, hand in hand.

Each spoonful whispers, secrets abound,
In a dish of happiness, we've finally found.
The pathway to joy, soft and sweet,
In a creamy realm, we dare to meet.

Waffle Cone Wonders

A waffle cone boat in a ocean of cream,
Setting sail on a sugary dream.
Flavors collide like stars in the night,
With a cherry on top, everything's right.

Every crunchy bite brings a giggle or two,
A symphony of tastes in a frosty hue.
Exploring the realms of sweet delight,
In the world of cones, all feels so bright.

Creamy Epiphanies Under Stardust

Under twinkling skies, I found a scoop,
A galaxy flavored, an icy loop.
With sprinkles of laughter, joy on my tongue,
I sang to the stars, a melody sprung.

Chocolate rivers flowed, a sweet, tasty stream,
In the land of delight, I dared to dream.
Each bite a portal, to giggles and glee,
In the frosty wonder, I felt so free.

A cherry on top, a crown for my wit,
In frosty bliss, my troubles would sit.
With cones like crowns and spoons like scepters,
To rule this kingdom, my sugar receptors.

So here's to the moments wrapped in delight,
Where every mouthful feels purely right.
In cones of rich cream, the laughter did bloom,
In a world of joy, there's always more room.

The Flavor of Forgotten Dreams

Once in a dream, I chased a scoop,
That danced on clouds, an icy troupe.
Mint chills and warmth made me giggle
As icy delights began to wiggle.

Sorbet sunsets and caramel sighs,
With every taste, my spirits arise.
I spooned through the laughter, a fun little chase,
In each sugary swirl, I found my place.

Flavors of childhood swirled in the night,
Strawberry wishes took on their flight.
The magic of sweetness, a wink from the past,
In the frozen embrace, my troubles surpassed.

So raise up your spoons, and let's make a toast,
To creamy adventures, let's celebrate most.
In the flavor of dreams, we find what we seek,
With giggles and joy, oh so unique.

Churning Confessions in a Bowl

In a bowl of secrets, I find my fears,
Churning them softly, with giggles and tears.
With scoops of truth piled high to the brim,
I sprinkle on fun, and start to grin.

Each flavor a story, each topping a tale,
A fudge-covered memory that never goes stale.
I dive in with spoons, as laughter erupts,
In this creamy chaos, my heart interrupts.

Whipped cream confessions like clouds in the sky,
I savor each moment, sipping pie on the sly.
With chocolate flurries and raspberry swirls,
I reveal all my quirks to the universe's pearls.

So here's to the scoops, the sweet and the silly,
To all the flavors that make life so frilly.
In bowls of enchantment, we find our reboot,
With churning confessions, we all follow suit.

Sugary Moments of Clarity

Sipping on sweetness, the world's so bright,
Each lick of caramel feels just right.
With fruity fun exploding with glee,
Every burst of flavor set my heart free.

Funky flavors rolled, like ideas galore,
In marshmallow dreams, I began to soar.
Toppings of laughter, sprinkles of cheer,
In this sugary world, everything's clear.

When life feels sticky, like melted fudge,
I dive in for comfort, I won't budge.
With every scoop, I rediscover my smile,
These sugary moments are truly worthwhile.

So gather your friends and savor the night,
In bowls of happiness, we take flight.
For every scoop shared whispers, 'You're right,'
In sugary moments, our souls take delight.

The Scoop of Spirit

In a world so sweet and bright,
A scoop can bring delight.
With sprinkles piled on high,
Who needs a reason why?

A cone that melts away,
Like worries of the day.
Each flavor holds a tale,
In every frosty gale.

The laughter with each lick,
Life's troubles seem to trick.
Chocolate, cherry, or mint,
In joy, we find a hint.

So gather 'round, my friends,
The fun never truly ends.
In every creamy swirl,
We find our little world.

Vanilla Visions

Vanilla dreams, oh what a sight,
Swaying softly in the light.
A creamy cloud, or is it fate?
It's never too late to celebrate!

With every scoop comes giggles too,
Who knew such joy was found in food?
A cone in hand, we run and play,
Sweeter than any ballet.

Whipped cream smiles upon our faces,
In this world, we find our places.
Each lick's a step in a dancing spree,
Chasing cones, just you and me.

So raise your spoons and toast the day,
Let's sprinkle joy in every way.
For as long as ice cream's near,
We'll laugh and taste without a fear.

The Frosty Truth

In this world of endless quests,
Ice cream stands above the rest.
A scoop reveals the cosmic gig,
In waffle cones, our hearts grow big.

Dancing flavors, bright and bold,
Stories wrapped in sweet, untold.
Minty whispers and fruity cries,
Spreading joy under sunny skies.

Life's twists may leave us cold,
But a sundae warms the soul,
When darkness looms, just take a bite,
Ice cream turns the wrong to right.

So let's embrace this frosty truth,
For with each scoop, we find our youth.
Laughter echoes, worries cease,
In every cone, we seek our peace.

Beneath the Frosting

Beneath the frosting, layers hide,
Treasures waiting to be spied.
With every spoonful, joy will bloom,
Let friendship fill the chilly room.

A cherry on top for laughter's sake,
With smiles shared around the cake.
Creating moments in each bite,
A sprinkle here, makes everything right.

So here's to laughter, fun, and glee,
To every creamy jubilee.
No matter how the world may seem,
We find our bliss in every dream.

With spoons aloft and hearts aglow,
We'll savor sweetness, let it flow.
For in each scoop, the world feels grand,
Ice cream laughter, hand in hand.

Frosty Interludes

In a cone or in a cup,
Sweet joy fills every sup.
A cherry on top just for fun,
With every scoop, I've already won.

Melting moments, sticky hands,
Sprinkles falling like glittery sands.
Laughter echoes with each sweet bite,
Nothing else feels quite so right.

Flavor wars erupt like tales,
Mint vs. chocolate, oh how it pales.
I'll take them all, my heart won't sway,
As happiness drips along the way.

So bring the cones, the bowls, the laughs,
In creamy swirls, we'll craft our paths.
Life's a treat, let's indulge and play,
In frosty interludes, we'll stay.

Dipped in Dreams

Sundaes stacked, oh what a sight,
Whipped cream peaks, such pure delight.
Chocolate rivers, caramel falls,
In this land, nothing else enthralls.

Dip it once, dip it twice,
Every flavor's oh so nice.
A cone that jingles with delight,
Each little scoop is pure romance tonight.

A sprinkle here, a jolt of cheer,
Every bite, I hold dear.
Scoops of joy, what can I say?
In these dreams, I want to stay.

So grab a spoon, let's make a pact,
To savor sweetness, that's a fact.
With laughter flowing like a stream,
We live our days dipped in dreams.

Layers of Laughter

Oh, the layers stacked so high,
Like a pastry in the sky.
Banana splits with whipped delight,
In every scoop, we find our light.

Laughter bubbles, giggles tease,
Ice cream parties, oh, such ease.
Birthday cakes and fudge galore,
Each bite opens up a door.

A scoop for you, a scoop for me,
Sharing joy so happily.
Layered flavors, sweet elation,
In every cone, pure celebration.

So let's raise a cone and cheer,
For every flavor we hold dear.
In this fun, we'll surely find,
Layers of laughter intertwined.

Frozen Frames of Reference

In the freezer, a treasure trove,
Frozen frames of sweet love.
Minty fresh and berry bold,
Each scoop a story waiting to be told.

Craving joy on a sunny day,
We'll chase the troubles far away.
With every lick, a giggling spree,
Those frosty moments set us free.

Spoons in hand, let's make a mess,
A race to finish, who'll impress?
Drips and drops become our fate,
In this savored, frozen state.

So grab a buddy, let's indulge,
In scoops of laughter, we'll be engulfed.
Through every smile, we'll take a chance,
In frozen frames, we'll dance.

Frosty Reminders

In a cone, my worries fade,
A scoop to savor, a sweet cascaded.
Sprinkles dance like little stars,
Melting madness in chocolate bars.

When the world gets all too tough,
I lick the scoop, it's just enough.
A sundae piled high with cheer,
Tastes like laughter, bright and clear.

The fridge whispers of late-night dreams,
Chilled delight bursting at the seams.
Life's a bowl of minty fun,
With every bite, my troubles shun.

So here's to frosty, creamy glee,
A frolic through sweet jubilee.
With every scoop, I find my muse,
In every flavor, I cannot lose.

Swirls of Serenity

In the summer sun, I twirl and spin,
A waffle cone with a joyful grin.
Each flavor whispers tales to me,
Of ocean waves and jubilee.

Chocolate rivers, caramel hills,
Every scoop brings winter thrills.
I tell my thoughts to melting cream,
As happiness flows like a sunny dream.

Life's a scoop of pumped-up fun,
With every swirl, I've just begun.
A cherry on top, my heart's delight,
Savoring sweetness, day or night.

So let's conquer all with a frosty cheer,
Save the day with butter pecan here.
With each dreamy taste, I kindly find,
Pure joy and laughter intertwined.

Creamy Contemplations

As I ponder life's big quest,
I take a scoop; it's simply the best.
Rocky Road to the unknown path,
A flood of fudge, it makes me laugh.

With toppings piled high, I can't resist,
A cherry bomb, I feel so blessed.
Sunshine sprinkles make joy comply,
With every lick, I reach for the sky.

Oh, what a world of creamy dreams,
Where hope is served in frozen streams.
A pint of laughter, sweet and bright,
Chasing shadows away at night.

So here I sit with my frozen treat,
In this delectable, life-sweet feat.
With every spoonful, I softly muse,
Life is grand, and I cannot lose.

Bites of Bliss

I giggle with joy with each creamy bite,
A moment so perfect, everything's right.
My troubles dissolve like a scoop on heat,
Each flavor a treasure, oh what a treat!

From cookie dough to strawberry bliss,
In every cone, there's a sweet little kiss.
Life's too short for a single scoop,
I conquer my worries in a frosty loop.

Eventual spills lead to giggly glee,
Who knew that chaos brought so much spree?
With every cone, my heart does sing,
In the world of ice cream, I'm a king.

So raise your spoons, let's cheer out loud,
With each creamy sight, I feel so proud.
In bites of bliss, I find my bliss,
In this frozen world, I can't resist.

The Ice Cream Chronicles

In a cone, I'm feeling grand,
Chocolate rivers, ice cream land.
A scoop of joy on sunny days,
Waffle prisms, sugary ways.

Sprinkles rain like confetti bright,
Each flavor battles, a taste delight.
Minty fresh or berry sweet,
Melting faster, can't be beat!

A dash of nuts, a cherry on top,
Happy giggles, never stop.
Fudge drips down, a sticky race,
Laughter swirls in every place.

Turn the corner, what do I see?
More flavors shouting, "Pick me, pick me!"
Sundaes calling, "Life's a dream!"
Reality's sweet as ice cream!

Palate Explorations

Choco chip or minty bliss?
Choosing flavors is pure bliss.
Every scoop's a little trip,
Taste buds do a happy skip.

Rainbow sherbet, bright and bold,
Tales of summer, sweetly told.
A sprinkle here, a drizzle there,
Taste adventures everywhere!

Sipping sundaes, oh so neat,
Cone to hand, can't be beat.
A bite of happiness, oh my!
Lick it quick, let worries fly!

Exploring flavors, like a quest,
Each new scoop—oh what a fest!
Banana splits and cookie dough,
Wonders lie in every row!

Delighted by the Scoop

With every scoop, a giggle starts,
Sprinkled hopes and melted hearts.
Cone of joy in every hand,
Savor sweetness, taste the land.

Every flavor holds a tale,
Of summer nights, or a fruity gale.
Rocky road or vanilla pure,
No regrets when you're this sure!

Chocolate rivers are calling me,
A cherry bomb, oh, can't you see?
Drip and drop, what's that a mess?
Sweetest chaos, who could stress?

Beneath the sun, we find our way,
Joyful scoops at the end of the day.
Laughter echoes, empty bowls,
A treat for hearts, a munch for souls!

Garnished Moments

The scoop is round, a fluffy dome,
Each flavor feels like coming home.
Sprinkled joys and scoops divine,
A creamy hug, so sweet, so fine.

Drizzles dance on frosty peaks,
Every bite, pure bliss it speaks.
Cotton candy dreams at play,
On this journey, come what may.

Garnished moments, laughter shared,
In every cone, love declared.
Raise a scoop to skies so blue,
Celebrate the happy crew!

So here's to flavors, wild and free,
Licking joy, just you and me.
In the end, the world's so bright,
With every scoop, it feels just right!

The Soft Serve of Society

In a world so churned, it's plain to see,
Frosty delights are the key to glee.
Life scoops us up, then swirls around,
Sprinkles of joy on the ups and downs.

So grab your cone, let's take a ride,
With flavors bold, and friends beside.
We'll laugh and lick 'til the sun goes down,
In this creamy chaos, we'll never frown.

In Search of Sweetness

Wander the streets for a taste so fine,
Searching for cones, that sugary sign.
Chocolate or vanilla, oh what a plight,
Finding true bliss in a scoop of light.

With every slurp, we dance in delight,
Chasing our cravings, it feels so right.
Life's a buffet of flavors galore,
Happiness served, who could ask for more?

Profound Parfaits

Layers of wonder, a bowl in hand,
Each spoonful whispers, 'Isn't life grand?'
Mix it up, swirl it, don't hold back,
In sweet exploration, we find our track.

A fudge waterfall, a berry spree,
Every rich flavor, a ticket to glee.
In this parfait of joy, we craft our fate,
Each bite a laughter, it's never too late.

Creamy Connections

Meet me at the sundae, under the sun,
Where laughter flows, and troubles are none.
Sharing our flavors, the scoop's never small,
In this sweet union, we've got it all.

From cherry on top to the waffle base,
Friendships are strengthened with every taste.
In the laughter and mess, we find our way,
With a cone in hand, we seize the day.

The Spectrum of Sweetness

A scoop of joy, in a waffle embrace,
Melting smiles, in every sweet trace.
Chocolate oceans, strawberry skies,
Toppings rain down, in joyful surprise.

Sprinkles of laughter, and cherries so bright,
Frosty delights that make everything right.
While flavors dance in a colorful spree,
Who needs deep thoughts? Just give me a key!

Whipped cream mountains, a sugary peak,
With every bite, it's adventure we seek.
As spoons play melodies, and cones take flight,
In the realm of sweetness, everything's light.

Tasting Time

Tick-tock goes the flavor parade,
Scoops in hand, to the dance we invade.
Minty freshness, a twist of delight,
In this creamy chaos, we dance through the night.

Caramel rivers, a sticky sweet flow,
Each taste a memory, a vibrant tableau.
Banana splits spark trust in the day,
Who cares about worries when we can play?

A flick of the tongue, a giggle erupts,
In this frosty journey, we joyfully cup.
As laughter expands, like cones in the heat,
Tasting time, oh heavens, can't be beat!

Gelato and Gratitude

With each creamy scoop, I whisper a thanks,
To the artists of flavors and colorful pranks.
Coconut whispers and citrusy chimes,
Unraveling joy in delicious rhymes.

Every drip down a cone makes me grin,
As peachy sunsets begin the spin.
Fruity adventures, wild and absurd,
With every bite, unspoken words stirred.

Grateful for gelato, forever my muse,
In every flavor, a giggle to choose.
So raise your spoons high, let's toast to delight,
In this realm of sweetness, the future looks bright.

The Cone of Contentment

Upon the horizon, a cone appears,
Filled with joy and topped off with cheers.
Two scoops of laughter and drizzles of fun,
Life's better served cold, under warm sun.

Each crunchy bite, a celebration divine,
Melting away worries, one scoop at a time.
Facing challenges with sprinkles in hand,
Let's waffle our troubles, together we stand.

Chocolate chips wink, as rainbows unfold,
In our cone of contentment, happiness bold.
So grab a flavor, let giggles ensue,
In this sweet journey, it's just me and you.

Chilled Reflections

In a cone of joy I find,
Melting moments, one of a kind.
Sundaes bring a goofy cheer,
Worries vanish, no more fear.

Scoops of laughter, sprinkles bright,
Mix of flavors, pure delight.
Chasing cones on summer nights,
Frosty dreams, oh what a sight!

Cups and cones, we dance around,
Chasing each other on the ground.
Whipped cream clouds, we can't resist,
Silly flavors, we must persist!

Savoring joy with each cold bite,
Brain freezes turn into delight.
Whirl and twirl, let worries stream,
In this world, we laugh and scream.

Beneath the Cherry Top

Underneath that cherry bright,
Lies a scoop of pure delight.
Each bite giggles in my brain,
Sweet and soft like summer rain.

Chocolate rivers, strawberry hearts,
Life is better with sugary parts.
Friends gather, sharing the fun,
Chasing dreams, we always run.

Every swirl, a tale to tell,
In this scoop, we find our spell.
Sticky fingers, happy sighs,
Laughter bubbles, joy that flies!

So gather 'round, let's share a scoop,
Join the dance, a silly loop.
Beneath the cherry, take a seat,
In this moment, life is sweet!

A Sprinkle of Serendipity

A sprinkle here, a sprinkle there,
Oh look! Joy fills the air.
Ice cream dreams, in flavors bold,
Stories sweetened, tales retold.

Swirls of colors, laughter flows,
Each cone a treasure, who really knows?
Fudge and nuts, a tasty mix,
Life's a party, let's get our fix!

Every scoop, a surprise awaits,
Bursting smiles, open gates.
Float away on this frozen treat,
With every tongue, we feel the heat!

Waffle cones and happy dance,
In this moment, we take a chance.
Sprinkles fly, we feel the glee,
In this world, we're wild and free!

Savoring the Simple

Life's a scoop, it tumbles down,
In every town, we share a crown.
Scooping memories from the past,
Every flavor, we want to last.

Cones of happiness, go ahead!
Whipped cream piled, no need for bread.
Every taste a giggle found,
Joyful moments, round and round.

Chasing drips with childlike glee,
Every drop a memory.
In sticky fingers, laughter hides,
With every bite, the world collides.

So grab a scoop and join the fun,
In every flavor, we have won.
Simple joys as sweet as pie,
With each cold bite, let's touch the sky!

Chilled Pursuits

In a cone or a cup, it's a race,
Sprinting to savor each taste.
Chocolate, vanilla, or mint chip,
Life's little joys, with each lick and sip.

Crispy waffle, oh what a thrill,
Sprinkles on top, it's a sweetened chill.
Dip it in fudge, give it a swirl,
With each cold bite, my heart does twirl.

Sundaes stacked, a towering delight,
Friends gather round to share in the bite.
Giggling and dreaming, flavors unite,
In this frosty world, everything's bright.

With a cherry on top, I proclaim,
Happiness found, can't put it to shame.
In a world of chaos, it's the simplest goal,
To chase after scoops and savor the whole.

A Palette of Possibilities

Minty fresh or a berry bliss,
Every scoop feels like a kiss.
Swirls of colors, a vibrant show,
In frosty dreams, joy seems to flow.

From creamy vanilla to tangy zest,
In this frosty quest, I find my best.
Flavors collide like laughter in the air,
With every taste, I toss away care.

Can we count flavors, oh what a task?
With each unique blend, no need to ask.
A sprinkle of joy in every bite,
This cold adventure feels so right.

So never you doubt, indulge and explore,
In this chilly realm, there's always more.
With friends by my side, we take our time,
Savoring moments, all in a rhyme.

Flavorful Revelations

Coconut twist in a summer glow,
With every taste, it's a tasty show.
Pineapple upside-down, give it a whirl,
Each scoop ignites, my tongue does twirl.

Caramel rivers, rich and sweet,
Each bite a treasure, a delicious treat.
Cherry jubilee, let the good times roll,
In this dessert journey, I find my soul.

Taste buds dancing, a swirling spree,
Fruity and nutty, oh what a decree.
With every flavor, life's puzzles clear,
In icy escapes, there's nothing to fear.

So here's to the scoops that fill our hearts,
In every flavor, a new life starts.
With laughter and sweetness, we all can blend,
Chasing cold dreams, around every bend.

Delight in Every Bite

Rich chocolate fudge, it darkly gleams,
Each satisfied sigh fuels my sweet dreams.
Peanut butter swirls, creamy and bold,
With every spoonful, adventure unfolds.

Banana split, the perfect delight,
With whipped cream clouds, a heavenly sight.
Nuts and toppings, a delightful race,
In this symphony, I find my place.

Popsicles dance in the summer sun,
Savoring happiness, oh what fun!
Frosty delights, a whimsical ride,
In every scoop, I take joy in stride.

So gather 'round, my sweet-toothed friends,
Where ice cream flows, the laughter never ends.
With flavors of joy, we take our part,
In this freeze-frame of an open heart.

The Dessert of Existence

In a bowl of laughter, we all swirl,
Flavorful giggles, let our hearts unfurl.
Sprinkles of joy, a cherry or two,
Life's sweet concoction, tastes so true.

Spoons clink together, what's yours to share?
A scoop of madness, without a care.
Brain freeze moments, we all might face,
Yet under the sun, we find our place.

The ice cream melts, like worries dissolve,
In each creamy bite, our dreams resolve.
Laughter erupts, like soda on cue,
Blissful reminders of what we can do.

So grab your cone, and let's take a ride,
With each delightful scoop, together we glide.
In this dessert frenzy, we savor the day,
With every sweet moment, we giggle and play.

Chill of Joy and Sorrow

In a freezer packed tight, my worries reside,
With each frosty treat, I take them for a ride.
Scoops of delight, with chocolate so dark,
Mix in the sprinkles, it hits just the mark.

Sundaes of joy, with sorrow on top,
A blend of emotions, we'll never stop.
In every drip, a story unfolds,
From sticky fingers to memories of gold.

We laugh through the mess, as flavors collide,
Each silly moment is where we confide.
Life's bittersweet blend, like sorbet's sharp bite,
Finding comfort in sweetness, feels oh so right.

As we savor the chill, let the world melt away,
In cups of delight, we'll always stay.
A mantra unfolds, as we giggle with glee,
For in this frosty world, we're truly free.

A Sweet Scoop of Existence

Scooping up joy, from a carton so wide,
A parade of flavors marching with pride.
Whipped cream mountains, parade like a dream,
In this creamy landscape, we plot and scheme.

Pass me the sprinkles, add some flair,
Each twist and turn is beyond compare.
We laugh at the mess, as scoops start to fly,
In this playful chaos, we'll reach for the sky.

A spoonful of sorrow, a dash of sweet glee,
In this carnival treat, I'm happy to be.
With waffle cone dreams tackling the sun,
Who knew that some ice cream could be so fun?

So raise your cones high, let the flavors unite,
In each drippy moment, everything's right.
We'll savor each scoop, 'neath the sky so blue,
For in this dessert, life's the best kind of brew.

Melting Moments of Joy

Life's a scoop of delight on a hot summer day,
With each frosty drip, our troubles fade away.
Crispy cones bursting, like laughter so loud,
In this whipped cream wonderland, we're all so proud.

Flavors collide, like our quirky array,
Marshmallow mysteries, we find our way.
Slips and slides on the path made of fudge,
In this sticky adventure, we'll never begrudge.

As the sun sets low, and the cones start to drip,
We gather together, for a sweet friendship trip.
A squirt of laughter, a sprinkle of cheer,
In these melting moments, we hold dear.

So share every scoop, let warm smiles combine,
In the laughter of sweetness, our hearts intertwine.
For in this grand dessert, what we seek is so pure,
Joy floats in our bowls, that we all can endure.

www.ingramcontent.com/pod-product-compliance
Lightning Source LLC
Chambersburg PA
CBHW072217070526
44585CB00015B/1377